W9-CZV-316

Follow That Map!

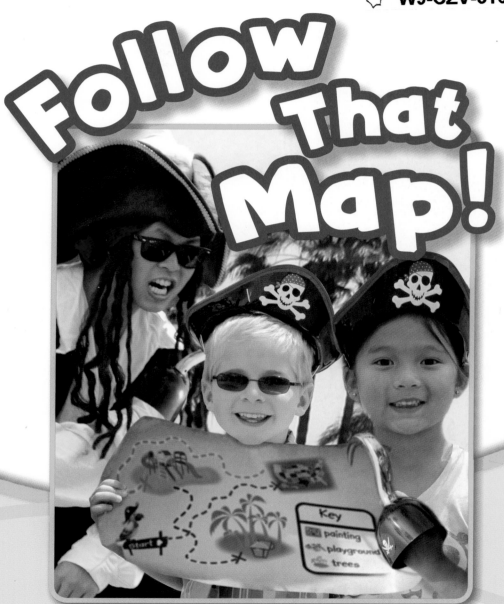

Sharon Coan, M.S.Ed.

It is a **party**.

We play games.

We have a **treasure** hunt.

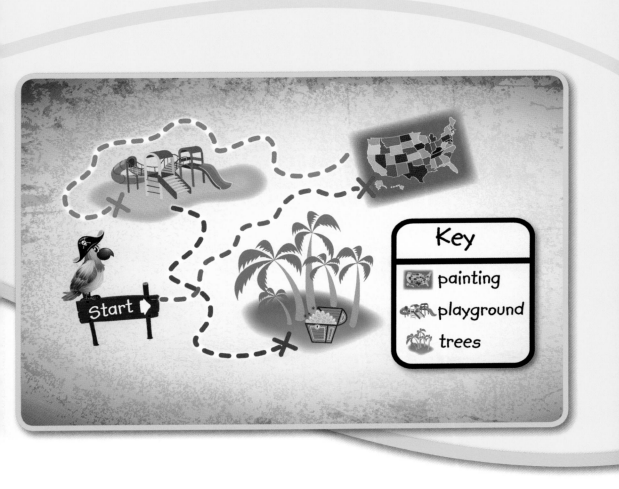

We use a **map**.

We follow the map.

We run to the first place.

We look for treasure.

The treasure is not
here.

We run to the second place.

We look for treasure.

The treasure is not
here.

We run to the third place.

We look for treasure.

The treasure is here!

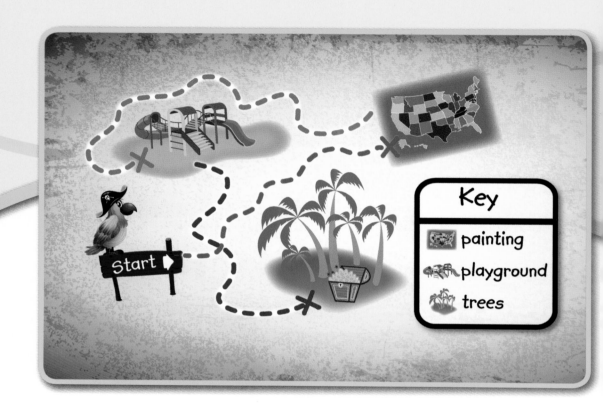

Key
painting
playground
trees

We used the map.

We found the
treasure!

Hide It!

1. Hide a treasure.

2. Make a map to find it.

3. Give the map to friends.

4. See if they can find the treasure.

Glossary

map—a picture that shows a place

party—a fun time with food and games

treasure—a thing that is special or important

Index

Your Turn!

The treasure is books. What is your favorite treasure? Draw a picture.

Consultants

Shelley Scudder
Gifted Teacher
Broward County Schools

Caryn Williams, M.S.Ed.
Madison County Schools
Huntsville, AL

Publishing Credits

Conni Medina, M.A.Ed., *Managing Editor*
Lee Aucoin, *Creative Director*
Torrey Maloof, *Editor*
Lexa Hoang, *Designer*
Stephanie Reid, *Photo Editor*
Rachelle Cracchiolo, M.S.Ed., *Publisher*

Image credits: Cover, pp. 3, 7, 9–11, 18, 23 (top), 24 Lexa Hoang; pp.4, 6, 8, 13–15, 22–23 (left) Jane Rahman; Backcover, pp.2, 12, 17, 23 (right) Stephanie Reid; p.19 Teacher Created Materials.

Teacher Created Materials
5301 Oceanus Drive
Huntington Beach, CA 92649-1030
http://www.tcmpub.com
ISBN 978-1-4333-7347-3
© 2014 Teacher Created Materials, Inc.